The Collaboration Kit

LYNNE STURTEVANT

CONTENTS

SECTION 1 – COLLABORATION BASICS

Collaboration can be the easiest, most effective and least expensive way to quickly produce a new tour or event – but only if you work with the right partner.

Potential Benefits

- **Collaborations are Temporary** – Collaborating is a trial period for both parties. There is no long-term commitment. You come together for a single project which means there is a clear beginning and a clear end to the relationship. You find out if you like working together and whether you can make money or achieve other goals. If it doesn't work for whatever reason, you're not stuck with your partner. Of course, they're not stuck with you either.

- **New Approaches and Fresh Ideas** – Many of us in local history and tourism work alone. Coming up with new ideas can be quite a challenge. Intellectual cross-pollination, discussing possibilities and sharing the workload with a collaboration partner can be fun, stimulating and lucrative. It can also help reduce the burnout factor. Collaborations don't always have to result in something brand new. A partner may suggest ways you can expand or update programs you are already offering or see new solutions to old problems.

- **Bridging the Skill Gap** – Look for a partner who has different skills and talents. Perhaps you're an idea generating machine but have a hard time actually getting programs off the ground. Or maybe you love to write but freeze if you have to speak to an audience. When you find the right person or organization with whom to collaborate, both you and your new partner extend your ranges. Two local historians may butt heads over program details. However, a local historian and a freelance guide who is a wiz at online marketing can be a pair to draw to.

- **Expanding Your Audience** – You and your partner bring more than your skill sets to the table;

you bring your respective audiences. This can be of great benefit to both of you, especially if one of your goals is to attract new customers. In fact, the size and demographic makeup of a potential partner's audience should be a prime element in your decision of whether or not to join forces. Ideally the collaboration will allow both of you to offer your audiences something new and to expand your respective reaches in terms of newsletter subscribers, members, contributors, volunteers, Facebook fans, Twitter followers, etc.

- **Pooling Resources and Sharing Risks** – What's preventing you from developing and offering great new programs? No staff or volunteers? No money? Do you need special equipment or some type of technical assistance? Is your lack of access to certain people, places or information sources holding you back? Collaborating with the right partner can bring programs that seemed out of reach into the realm of the possible.

- **Prospering Beyond the Program** – A successful collaboration may lead to future projects, but it can also benefit you in other ways. You'll increase your visibility and expand your professional network. You may gain on-the-job experiences that enhance your credentials. There might also be other ways you and your partner can work together. For example, maybe you can spruce up their Facebook page in exchange for help with web design.

Collaboration Candidates

Excellent collaboration candidates include:

- Museums – Don't overlook small or regional museums that may be more open to collaboration than larger institutions.
- Historic attractions including museum houses
- Visitors' Bureaus
- Downtown revitalization organizations – see **Case Study 2**
- Historical societies – see **Case Study 3**
- Preservation groups
- Merchants' groups
- Neighborhood associations
- Independent tour operators
- Freelance guides
- Public historians
- Chambers of Commerce

Here are a few less obvious candidates along with program suggestions:

- Libraries – see **Case Study 1**

- Antique shops and vintage clothing stores – Visit your local merchants and find out what periods and types of items they specialize in. Could you collaborate and offer a program on Victorian table manners and dining etiquette? The antique shop owner could explain what the various forks, knives and other utensils were for. Maybe your audience would enjoy learning about day-to-day life during a particular period. Your antique dealer could bring in an assortment of everyday items, things that are no longer used but were once indispensable. Could you offer a history of hats fashion show? Many baby boomers would enjoy a program on vintage toys. Use your imagination and find out what the shop owner would suggest.

- Genealogy clubs – Anyone local you could partner with for a workshop on cleaning tombstones? How about a cemetery tour examining gravestone symbolism from various periods?

- Garden clubs – Do you have a county extension service? Are there master gardeners or a landscape company that might like to partner with you? If you can be outside, how about heirloom gardening, victory gardens or growing colonial herbs? If it's winter, a program on cooking with herbs or the language of flowers might draw a crowd.

- Wedding and event planners – Recreate a 1950s wedding. Talk about the roots of wedding superstitions. Why do we tie old shoes to the car or need something borrowed and something blue?

- Bars – How about the history of cocktails complete with samples? Discuss how tastes and styles have changed over the decades or focus on an alcohol-intense period such as the 1920s. Offer a guided tour of historic taverns with local prohibition stories.

- Restaurants, caterers, cooking shops and schools – Offer a cooking demonstration or, even better, a hands-on cooking class. Prepare and sample typical dishes from different periods. Or focus exclusively on one dish such as chicken soup through the decades.

- Photographers – Partner with a freelancer or studio and offer a few basic classes followed by a photo safari to a historic neighborhood.

Working with Competitors

Don't overlook attractions, organizations or freelancers in a neighboring city or across town. People you think of as competitors might be outstanding collaboration partners. Here are few ideas to help you think about how this could work.

- Partner with another attraction or group of attractions to create a local history trail. Give it a great name and market it together. Create a history scavenger hunt that links your attractions via the clues.

- Line up three historic venues – houses, museums, hotels – and offer a series of formal dances, concerts or costume parties that represent three key periods in your town's past. Sell tickets to all three events as a single pass and present it as part of your town's historic "social season."

- If a formal dance would not appeal to your target audience, how about a dinner or hors d'oeuvres tasting held on three different nights at three different venues, again each representing a different phase of your town's history?

- Not interested in food, costumes or music? Could you tell a large story from three different points of view in three different venues, a variation on the history trail concept? The World War II home front in Mayfield as experienced by housewives, businesspeople and school children.

Approaching Potential Partners

Sometimes you know exactly who you'd like to be your partner. Maybe you think they'd be great people to work with, you want to hold a program in their wonderful venue or you hope to gain access to their audience or customer base. Before you approach them, do your homework. Take a look at their website and mission statement. See what kind of programs they've offered in the past and what's coming up. Can you develop a concept that dovetails with their specialty?

Identify and spell out exactly what they are likely to gain by working with you. What do you bring to the table? Expertise? Experience? Do you have a large following or audience? Do you have access to off-limits locations or material? What do you expect them to contribute? You need to know the answers to these questions before you approach your potential partner.

When you're ready, get the conversation started. Reach out and tell them you are looking for ways you might work together. Listen very closely to their ideas and concerns. Be open to the possibility that you may need to rethink your plans.

What if You're Approached?

What if the tables are turned and someone approaches you about collaborating? Ask yourself the same questions you would expect your potential partner to consider. What's in it for you? Access to a new audience?

New people to work with? What do they expect you to do? How much time do you think this will take? How much risk is there? If something doesn't seem right, don't ignore that feeling.

Red Flags

Not all collaborations lead to successful programs and uplifting experiences. Some are disastrous. Often, when viewed in retrospect, it's clear problems existed from the very beginning of the arrangement. Here are a few things to watch out for.

- Partners with unrealistic expectations
- Partners who drop the ball early in the process
- Partners with really bad ideas
- Partners who are micromanagers
- Partners who are overly emotional
- Prima donnas
- Partners who bring nothing to the table

Depending on the types of organizations involved, both you and your potential partner may face internal obstacles such as reticent and overly bureaucratic boards, staff problems and turf battles. These kinds of issues can sink your program. You and your partner need to be honest with each other and go in with your eyes open.

Operational Considerations

Pulling it all together involves making decisions in advance and agreeing with your partner about logistics, budgets, tasks, responsibilities and timelines.

- What is the program's ultimate goal? Good turnout? Big payday? Positive press coverage? You won't know whether you've achieved your goal if you don't establish what it is. You and your partner will probably have different sub-goals. Make sure these don't conflict.

- Who is in charge overall? Decide this before a conflict arises.

- Select the date, time and secure the venue or venues. Will the program run more than once?

- Identify all program costs and decide who is responsible for what.

- What price, if any, will you charge for tickets or admission?

- How much do you hope to clear after expenses? How many people need to attend for you to reach that goal?

- Income and profit are not the same thing. How and when will you split the proceeds? Who gets what? What happens if you lose money?

- Identify the necessary steps and tasks and assign responsibility and a due date to each one. For example, who is responsible for printing programs, tickets, posters, etc.? When will that be completed?

- Do you have contingency plans in case of bad weather or illness of key players?
- What is your marketing plan? Newsletters, websites, social media, flyers, posters, rack cards, TV, radio, newspaper, press releases, public speaking, blog posts? Who does what, when and how often?
- Identify everyone who will be working at the actual event.

Get It in Writing

You do not need to have a formal contract. A memo that the main parties sign off on is enough. An example of a simple yet effective agreement follows the case studies.

Post Event Analysis

After the tour, program or event, have a chat with your partner. How did things go? Was turnout better or worse than you anticipated? Did you make or lose money? How about other goals, such as adding names to your mailing lists or attracting new volunteers? Were those targets met?

What lessons did you learn? Should the event have been longer, shorter or offered at a different time? Did you miss critical steps or did you waste time or money on unnecessary steps? What kind of feedback did you get?

Will you and your partner work together again? Will you offer the same program? What will you change?

SECTION 2 – REGIONAL THINKING AND LINKING

In order to find ways to collaborate with other people and organizations, sometimes you have to think way outside the box.

Collaborating for Marketing and Learning

A group of small towns in southern Ontario, Canada is participating in a fascinating collaboration experiment called Tweetfolk Tours. Created and managed by a local social media firm, the program is designed to promote local businesses and attractions and it is based entirely on Twitter.

Each Tweetfolk Tour includes two components: an organization or business willing to host an event and the Tweetfolk, which is what the tour participants are called.

Potential hosts – restaurants, wineries, museums, historic houses, shops, local tour companies, bakeries –

apply to the social media firm that coordinates the tours. To be selected, a host must meet the following criteria:

- It must be a local business or organization, not a franchise or part of a chain.
- It must be active on Twitter, which means it must have a track record of tweeting on a regular basis. Opening an account simply to qualify as a host does not work.
- It must offer a complimentary experience-based event that lasts an hour to two hours.

The experience must be exclusive, not something anyone can get any day of the week. It does not have to be complex, however. A restaurant might offer a tour of the kitchen followed by a dessert tasting. A nature preserve might offer an introduction to bird identification followed by a make-your-own birdhouse workshop.

The social media firm reveals the location of each Tweetfolk Tour on Twitter three – five days prior to the event. Space is limited and the Tweetfolk register as quickly as they can, also over Twitter. The tours always fill up, often within minutes. The Tweetfolk agree to show up on time and to bring their smartphones.

During the event, the Tweetfolk generate a storm of live tweets. They describe what they are doing, talk about what fun they are having, rave about the food and post dozens of photos. An outside observer who happened in on the event would see a roomful of people looking intently at their phones. She would probably assume they were disengaged, lost in their own worlds. But, as the old saying goes, appearances can be deceiving. The Tweetfolk are not disconnected from their surroundings; they are intimately connected to the location, to each other and to the people near and far who are following along on Twitter.

Not only does this innovative program generate valuable word-of-mouth referrals for the hosts, local people are discovering great businesses in their own backyards.

The Tweetfolk benefit too. They are forging new friendships and business connections. People who were hesitant about using Twitter or just didn't understand it are learning about its potential as a marketing channel. Throughout the events the Tweetfolk help each other improve their Twitter skills, recommend interesting accounts to follow and share tips to make tweeting easier and more fun.

Who knows what types of lucrative collaborations might develop between people and businesses who meet in this environment?

Collaborating to Staff an Event

What do you do if you have an idea for a great new program, tour or event but you don't have enough staff to pull it off? Many people would file the great idea away and reluctantly move on to something smaller and more achievable. There is another way to approach the problem, however. Consider collaborating with a community theater or acting group. If there is no community theater in your area, consider approaching the high school drama club or a scout troop working on Celebrating Community, Public Speaking, Local History or Theater merit badges.

Actors can give formal presentations, participate in living history demonstrations, serve as guides and docents, or be hosts at open house type events where visitors travel from stop to stop.

Perhaps the most effective way to use their talents is to have them portray real historical figures or composite characters. They can participate in special programs such as a Colonial wedding recreation or give firsthand accounts of significant events. For example, your actor might tell visitors about her experiences helping fugitive slaves travel along the Underground Railroad or describe being physically attacked for being a Suffragette.

However you use them, actors add fresh energy, an element of entertainment and the potential for audience engagement many programs lack. Here are a few more great reasons to give this approach a try.

- Actors are more versatile than reenactors. Reenactors may spend months or years researching a particular period and developing a specific character. Actors, on the other hand, are not locked into a single era or persona. They can portray a wide range of people from various periods and places.

- Working with actors gives you the ability to control your program via a script. You are both the stage director and the playwright. You choose the subject and write the material, decide how it will be presented, who will say what, and set the program's length.

- Your regular volunteers may be uncomfortable with the idea of portraying characters. For some the mere suggestion may be enough to induce paralyzing stage fright and a refusal to participate.

- In most cases actors will do a better job portraying characters than volunteers will. Actors tend to be more relaxed in front of people. They have stage presence. They know how to get into character. Plus they will learn their lines faster and are likely to stick to the script. No wandering off into uncharted territory.

- Actors are used to taking direction. Volunteers may be hurt or offended if you suggest changes to their performances.

- Your local theater has costumes and someone on their team probably knows how to alter them. They may also have a good supply of props. Actors are comfortable wearing costumes and know how to use props effectively.

- If you keep an open mind, you may discover your actors – even if they are high school students or scouts – have suggestions on how to improve your program. Ask for their ideas.

- Working with local theatrical groups helps them! There are never enough acting opportunities, especially in small towns. Participating in your program gives actors valuable experiences they can add to their resumes.

- And last, but certainly not least, good collaborations almost always lead to other projects. Working with new people and groups can expand the audience for your future programs too.

Remember, when you work with young people, you often connect with their universe of parents, grandparents, friends, coaches and teachers.

SECTION 3 – CASE STUDIES

The following four case studies illustrate different ways organizations and individuals can work together. Collaborations do not have to be elaborate, overly complex arrangements. **Case Study 4**, which chronicles an effort that ultimately failed, is included because learning what doesn't work can be as valuable as learning what does.

Case Study 1: Library Summer Reading Tour

Parties:

Library – the Marietta (Ohio) Public Library; Friends – the Friends of the Marietta Library, a private organization that raises funds for special projects; HM - Hidden Marietta, an independent tour operator.

Goal:

The Library participates in the Collaborative Summer Library Program to promote reading by children, teens and adults. Each year there is a new theme with corresponding slogans for the three target groups. Participating libraries have access to colorful branded items such as signs, logos, stickers and reading certificates. They are encouraged to develop local activities that relate to that year's theme.

Librarians had no problem coming up with program ideas for children and teens. Finding an activity that would appeal to adult readers, however, was proving to be a challenge.

Program Overview:

In the spring the Library contacted HM to explore the feasibility of developing two walking tours related to that year's theme, which was Dig into Reading. One tour would be offered in June; the second – with a different itinerary – would be offered in July.

The Friends agreed to compensate HM for designing and running the tours so the Library could offer the experience to their adult patrons free of charge. The amount allocated for each tour was $250.00. There was a limit of 50 participants per tour.

Coming up with concepts that worked with Dig into Reading was easy. Library staff and HM decided the overall theme would be Dig into Local History.

Marietta was built on and around several ancient Indian mounds. HM had already developed a guided exploration of the mounds. The tour, called Ancient

Earthworks, was generally offered only to private groups so most people were unaware of it. The parties selected Ancient Earthworks for the June program.

For the July program, the parties shifted their attention to downtown. HM developed a new tour called the History Hunt which focused on the back alleys and brick passageways of downtown. The program was promoted as a soft urban archeology/detective experience.

Time Frame:

Lead time was approximately four weeks; event duration was two hours.

Main Tasks:

- The Ancient Earthworks tour was ready. No additional preparation was needed.
- The new History Hunt tour had to be researched, designed and written.
- Collateral material such as posters, flyers and tickets had to be created.
- Both events had to be promoted.

Roles:

- Friends served as the program sponsor and funding source.
- The Library promoted the program, made media appearances, issued press releases, took reservations and checked people in at the tour starting point.

- HM provided historical background, wrote the tour material, handled logistics and conducted the tours.

Branding:

The library used the branded materials supplied by the Collaborative Summer Library Program.

Costs:

As stated above, Friends contributed $500 to compensate HM.

Attendance:

One hundred people, the maximum number, 50 in June and 50 in July, participated in the programs.

Improvements for Year Two:

Everything went so well the first year, the parties decided to work together again the following summer.

The next year's summer reading theme for adults was Literary Elements. The children's and teens' slogans (Fizz, Boom, Read! and Spark a Reaction) had scientific slants so HM and the Library turned to the four elements of the classical world – earth, air, fire and water – for inspiration.

Marietta is located at the confluence of two rivers and has been flooded repeatedly. Unfortunately, several disastrous fires have also blazed through town. HM created a new tour called Fire and Water: Agents of Change, an examination of how these forces shaped the cityscape.

Rather than offering two different programs as in the previous year, the parties decided to offer Fire and Water twice, once in June and again in July. They added visual aids in the form of vintage photographs of downtown fires, floods and buildings in various stages of construction and destruction. The Library printed the images and made them into handouts. Having a packet of pictures to refer to as they walked the tour route deepened the experience for the adult readers.

Once again, both sessions were full.

Summary:

This is an outstanding example of a program that works for everyone. The Friends enabled 200 library patrons to participate in new programs. The Library provided their adult readers with interesting experiences that fit with the summer reading themes. HM was nicely compensated for conducting four pleasant afternoon excursions. And best of all, the tour participants enjoyed looking at their hometown in different ways.

Case Study 2: Downtown Revitalization Group Fundraiser

Parties:

MMS – the local downtown revitalization organization; HM – Hidden Marietta, an independent tour operator; CVB – the local Convention and Visitors' Bureau; downtown building owners; community volunteers.

Goal:

To create an ongoing annual program that draws people into downtown, MMS's target area. The program should focus on history and preservation. It should highlight the positive nature of MMS's role in the community and be a significant fundraiser for the organization.

Program Overview:

For one afternoon, tour participants have access to areas of historic downtown buildings that are normally off-limits. They travel on their own and visit the stops in whatever order they like. A host at each location provides details about the structure's history.

Time Frame:

Lead time was approximately three months; event duration was three hours plus two hours of post-tour social time.

Main Tasks:

- Scouting buildings and convincing property owners to participate
- Performing background research on the various locations
- Recruiting and training volunteers
- Producing collateral material such as posters, programs, tickets, etc.
- Promoting the program

Roles:

- MMS served as program sponsor, secured permission to enter five buildings, covered all program and promotion costs, provided liability insurance for all venues and HM, issued press releases, made media appearances, recruited volunteers.
- HM recommended specific buildings, provided historical background on selected buildings, provided historic photos, recruited volunteers, wrote scripts for and trained volunteers, promoted the program to HM's customers and large social media base.
- CVB provided design assistance, helped with printing, promoted the program to CVB's customers and large social media base.

Branding:

- When the program was offered for the first time, the working title was Hidden Rooftops, Secret Gardens. Intriguing, but limiting. By changing it to Hidden Places, Secret Spaces, the parties retained the mystery but gave themselves plenty of latitude as to what could be included on the tour.

- An intern working with MMS designed a logo, poster, program, tickets and an event map based on vintage images supplied by HM. Everyone liked the look and feel of the materials so in the second year only minimal tweaks were needed. The files were updated with the new date, addresses, building details, etc.

- By using the same program name, logo, colors and other visual elements on all marketing and customer pieces, the parties are establishing a clear and consistent brand identity for the event.

Issues from Year One:

- Volunteer building hosts did not have enough background information about their buildings and did not fully engage with the visitors in some cases.

- People traveled the tour route in groups, clustering at the venues, creating bottlenecks and making it impossible to hear.

- At the end of the program everyone just drifted off and went home.

Improvements in Year Two:

- MMS and HM provided training, orientation and a private tour for volunteers a week before the event.
- There were two volunteers at most buildings, one to speak and one to control traffic flow, which alleviated the bottlenecks customers experienced in the first year.
- Volunteers had notes and lots of historic photos to help them explain the significance of the sites and make the past real for the guests.
- Volunteers were encouraged to wear historic costumes. All volunteers had "official" name tags, which made them feel they were part of a team.
- The parties held a reception at The Adelphia, another historic building, at the end of the event so people could mingle, chat and relax. Turnout was great.
- HM developed a simple questionnaire that asked people what else they'd like to do and collected email addresses.

Costs:

Costs for this program are minimal. Printing, limited use of Facebook ads, snacks for the reception (second year only).

- Year 1 – approximately $300.
- Year 2 – approximately $250.

Attendance, Gross Receipts and Splits:

- Year 1 – 157 people at $15 each totaling $2355
- Year 2 – 337 people at $15 each totaling $5055 – a 114% increase
- HM received $5 per participant. The balance went to MMS.

Summary:

History is part of Marietta's DNA. It is mentioned over and over by both out-of-town visitors and local people looking for new and different experiences. The historic downtown is a key component in the town's broader story. The individual buildings and the aspects of the past they illuminate are largely unexplored territory. This popular, profitable, and easy-to-run program will provide excellent returns for years to come.

Case Study 3: Nonprofit Group Historic Home Tour

Parties:

DVV – a downtown promotion group; The Society - the county historical society; HM – Hidden Marietta, an independent tour operator; downtown building owners; community volunteers.

Goal:

To create a new annual event that draws people into downtown. This is an open house type event that features some of the oldest buildings in Cambridge. The buildings are currently used as offices, the county historical society and one private home. The program should highlight the town's history and be a significant fundraiser for DVV and the Society.

Program Overview:

This tour follows the same format as the Hidden Places, Secret Spaces event described in **Case Study 2**. For one evening, participants have special permission to visit historic downtown buildings. Although four are offices, many people have not been inside. If they have been inside, they have not felt free to explore the premises. There are also many who have not visited the historical society even though it is open to the public. The one private residence on the tour should be particularly appealing.

Participants travel on their own and visit the stops in whatever order they like. A host at each location provides details about the structure's history. Each location serves complimentary light refreshments. The tour runs from 5 – 7pm when a street festival with food, crafts and music starts one block away. The historic home tour is a prelude to that event and links to it thematically.

Time Frame:

Lead time was approximately six weeks; event duration was two hours.

Main Tasks:

- Scouting buildings and convincing building owners to participate
- Performing background research on the various locations
- Recruiting and training volunteers
- Creating collateral materials such as posters, programs, tickets, etc.
- Promoting the program
- Staffing the stops during the event

Roles:

- DVV served as program sponsor, secured permission to enter five buildings, covered all program and promotion costs, provided liability insurance for all venues and HM, issued press releases, made media appearances, recruited volunteers.

- The Society provided historical background on selected buildings and provided historic photos.
- HM set up the tour logistics, wrote scripts for volunteers, created collateral material such as flyers, programs, tickets, etc., assisted at the tour, promoted the program to HM's customers and large social media base.

Branding:

The parties chose the name Harvest Home to link the tour to the Fall Festival, a community street party occurring the same evening. DVV also introduced the name "The Red Brick District" for the historic neighborhood that was being toured. Future branding activities will flow from those themes.

Costs:

Costs for this program are minimal. Printing was done in-house and there was a small cost associated with the refreshments. The total was about $30.

Attendance and Gross Receipts:

Thirty-two people at $10 each totaling $320. Receipts were split three ways between DVV, HM and the Society.

Summary:

Although turnout was not enormous, all parties were pleased. This is a new tour and customer feedback was overwhelmingly positive. The building and business owners had positive experiences as well. All in all, this was an excellent community event and should only get bigger and better with time.

Case Study 4: When Collaborations Fail - The Rise and Fall of the Victorian Funeral

Parties:

HM – Hidden Marietta, an independent tour operator; the Mansion – a Gothic Revival museum house; a funeral director; community volunteers

Goal:

To keep a popular program running when collaboration partners pulled out.

Background:

Early in the summer HM contacted the Mansion and offered to present a program on Victorian-era funeral practices and mourning etiquette. The Mansion's director accepted, and the program was scheduled for late October, close to Halloween. The parties agreed to split receipts 50/50.

HM then approached a local funeral director who had a large collection of antique mortuary paraphernalia and asked if he'd like to display some of his items at the program. He agreed. HM and the Mansion offered to share a portion of the receipts with the funeral director. He declined that offer.

The program was held in the Mansion's grand parlor. Mansion staff and HM dressed the room in mourning. The funeral director provided an amazing array of interesting objects including an antique coffin.

The Mansion's staff was overwhelmed by the turnout. Seating was limited and there were long lines of people waiting to get in. In an attempt to accommodate everyone, visitors were allowed to sit on the floor and stand at the back of the parlor and in the hallways. The program was offered twice. Attendance for the first session was 55; attendance for the second was 52, a total of 107. Admission was $10.

The First Crisis:

The following year, HM and the Mansion looked forward to repeating the popular and very lucrative program. Unfortunately, the funeral director withdrew less than two weeks before the program stating it was "too much trouble" to put his artifacts on display. The Mansion and HM pulled together what artifacts they could, decorated the parlor and went ahead with the program as planned. Only 39 people attended.

Based on the first season's turnout, the Mansion and HM were confident the public was interested in Victorian funeral practices. The parties also felt the Gothic house was the prefect venue for the program. They needed to find a different way to present the material, one that was interesting, engaging and did not rely too heavily on outside sources.

Back to the Drawing Board:

After much discussion, the parties decided to abandon the show and tell lecture format and create an immersive, interactive experience. Rather than confining the public to the parlor, costumed volunteers would escort small groups of visitors through the house.

They envisioned the program as a hybrid between a show and tell lecture, a traditional house tour and a play. HM created a fictional deceased person with a representative life story and cause of death. The goal was not to recreate a specific person's actual funeral. The parties wanted to illustrate what funerals during the late 19th century were like. They further wanted the customers to feel they had stepped back in time and been part of a real event. In addition to giving customers a broader experience of the Mansion, the format would allow the parties to accommodate a much larger total number of people.

In year three, which was the first year of the revised format, the Mansion agreed to add the dining room, sitting room and summer kitchen to the program. Each room was dressed in mourning with black draping and ribbons. Pictures and mirrors were covered, etc.

There was no shortage of volunteers wanting to serve as escorts and to be stationed around the house. The main draw for many – all of whom were women – was to wear a costume and play a historic role in the wonderful old house. Each volunteer played a specific family member who told a different part of the story. In the promotional material for the program, the Mansion invited the public to wear mourning attire. Many obliged.

Attendance and Receipts:

The first year of the new and improved version, the program ran for two afternoons over one weekend. Fifty-nine people attended. Customers said they loved the experience. The volunteers had a wonderful time playing their roles as well.

Due to the amount of time and effort needed to decorate the house, the parties decided to extend the program over two weekends for year four. The upstairs bedrooms were also added to the tour. Attendance jumped to 167.

They stayed with the two-weekend format for year five and raised the admission price from $10 to $13. That year 173 people attended. In year six the admission price was raised to $15. Attendance dropped to 123.

Some of the year six drop off may have been related to the price increase. However, many of those involved felt the problem was the program itself. Even though HM changed the details of the story each year, it had begun to feel stale. The Mansion is located in a small market and does not have a large potential audience to draw from. It was time to revamp once again.

The Year Seven Boondoggle:

By this time, the Mansion had a new director. He agreed the program needed to be updated. He decided to switch to a historically accurate re-enactment of a Civil War-era military funeral. HM, having no background or interest in the Civil War, bowed out. The Mansion assumed sole responsibility for the program. The Civil War Funeral was offered for one weekend. Total attendance was 19.

Summary:

The story of the rise and fall of the Victorian Funeral contains three critical lessons.

The first relates to the danger of becoming too dependent on a collaboration partner. If the Mansion and HM hadn't been determined to find a way to make the program work in the second year, the funeral director's departure would have doomed the event. In fact, it was his departure that allowed the successful new format to emerge.

The theme of a losing a collaboration partner arose again in the seventh and final year, but with a less positive outcome. HM had handled most of the tasks associated with planning and offering the funeral including the critical job of recruiting, coordinating and communicating with volunteers. As a result, most of the volunteers upon whom the program depended did not have independent relationships with anyone at the Mansion. When the director decided to forge on alone, not only did crucial tasks fall by the wayside, the volunteer base evaporated as well.

The second lesson relates to the danger of not knowing or understanding your target audience. The Civil War program did not appeal to the Mansion's mainly female customer base who enjoyed learning about etiquette, fashion, jewelry, how the house was dressed in mourning and other matters that occupied women during the Victorian era.

And finally, if programs are to survive, they must be constantly re-imagined and refreshed. Nothing lasts forever. Sometimes even the events we love the most need to be laid to rest.

SECTION 4 – SAMPLE AGREEMENT

The following agreement covers the program described in **Case Study 2: Downtown Revitalization Group Fundraiser**. Party A is the downtown organization and HM is an independent tour operator.

Program Description –

For one afternoon tour participants have access to areas of historic downtown buildings that are normally off-limits. They travel on their own and visit the stops in whatever order they like. A host at each location provides details about the structure's history.

Roles and responsibilities –

Party A –

- Secures access to five historic downtown buildings to serve as venues
- Covers all program costs including paid promotion and advertising

- Arranges for the printing and distribution of all marketing materials including posters, programs, handouts and tickets
- Arranges volunteers to cover venues not covered by HM and to staff the reception table, sell tickets, collect money and handle customer questions before and during the program
- Provides liability insurance to all venues and HM

HM –

- Researches and writes blurbs and background information/stories on all venues and provides digital images when available
- Provides volunteers for two venues
- Promotes the event on the HM Facebook page, website and newsletter

Timeframe (with two months lead time) –

- Event date – May 16
- Venues confirmed – March 21
- Research completed and background information written – April 4
- Marketing materials completed and to printer – April 18
- Marketing materials distributed – April 25
- Volunteers onboard – April 25
- Volunteer training – May 9

Ticket Price and Revenue Splits –

Tickets are $15. No discounts for children or seniors. $5 of each ticket sold goes to HM. Party A retains the balance.

CONCLUSION

I sincerely hope you found this information useful. Collaboration opportunities are all around us, if we are open to the possibilities working with others may offer. Don't lose sight of your goals. Make sure your potential partner's objectives are the same as yours, or that they are at least complimentary. Watch out for red flags and get it in writing. Good luck!

Do you have questions? Was there a section or sections that weren't clear? Is there an area you'd like information (or more information) on? Feel free to send me an email. My contact information is in the Author Information section. Thanks for reading *The Collaboration Kit*.

Author Information

My tourism career began in 1986 when I started as a front-line travel agent. Eventually, I worked my way up to ownership of a thriving commercial agency in the heart of Washington, DC. I've escorted tour groups, taught at a travel school and conducted dozens of destination workshops. I was the marketing director of a tour operator specializing in Southeast Asia, represented the China International Travel Service and managed all travel programs for ASTA, the world's largest travel trade association.

After moving to the small town of Marietta, Ohio, I immersed myself in the world of local history and hyper-local tourism. I founded my own tour company. My first program was a ghost walk. The tour was so popular, I attracted the attention of The History Press, a traditional publishing house. The two books I wrote for them – ***Haunted Marietta: History and Mystery in Ohio's Oldest City*** and ***A Guide to***

Historic Marietta, Ohio – are available online and in bookstores nationwide.

The best part of my local history and tourism adventure was working with community groups. I collaborated with Main Street organizations, visitors' bureaus, county and state historical societies, a public library, downtown merchants' associations, hotels, restaurants, a college, a community theater and several attractions including historic houses, museums and even an old-fashioned riverboat. You'll find lots of local history tour and program ideas and other free resources at TheHistoryBiz.com.

I now live in Albuquerque, New Mexico and I'm excited to share the amazing things I'm learning about this beautiful state on my New Mexico history and travel blog. It's at HiddenNewMexico.com. You can keep up with everything else I'm doing at LynneSturtevant.com.

Thanks again for reading *The Collaboration Kit*. Do you have questions about the material? Was there a section or sections that weren't clear? Is there an area you'd like information (or more information) on? Feel free to contact me at Lpsturtevant@gmail.com or via the contact pages on any of my websites. I'd love to hear from you.

Books

Explore the world of local history and travel with Lynne Sturtevant. All titles are available on Amazon.

Create Successful Walking Tours

Whether you work in an historic house, a regional museum, a Main Street organization, for the Visitors' Bureau or run your own business, **Create Successful Walking Tours** will help you find appealing ideas for programs, show you how to design tours properly and market them effectively to the right audiences.

Create Successful Walking Tours covers how to choose the best theme and structure for your tour; what to do if you're completely out of program ideas; how to uncover the quirky details that will make your tour shine; how to design a logical itinerary; how to handle reservations, ticketing, equipment and customer questions; how to price your tour; how to staff your tour; how much to pay guides; how to promote your tour without breaking the bank; and how to avoid the myriad of potential tour day problems.

A Guide to Historic Marietta, Ohio

Welcome to Marietta, the elegant river city where Ohio's history begins. Explore ancient earthworks, stroll shady brick streets lined with glorious Victorian mansions, wander through museums, browse for antiques in the beautifully preserved downtown, kickback in a wide variety of restaurants and taverns or take a relaxing cruise down the scenic Ohio River. Venture into nearby West Virginia and visit Fenton, America's oldest art glass company; Blennerhassett Island where Aaron Burr hatched a plot against the US government; and Henderson Hall, the majestic great house of a former slave plantation – all within

15 miles of downtown Marietta. *A Guide to Historic Marietta, Ohio* will help you make the most of your time. It includes an overview of the area's rich history, maps, dozens of vintage and modern photos and descriptions of the best sites and attractions the region has to offer – including those most visitors miss.

Haunted Marietta: History and Mystery in Ohio's Oldest City

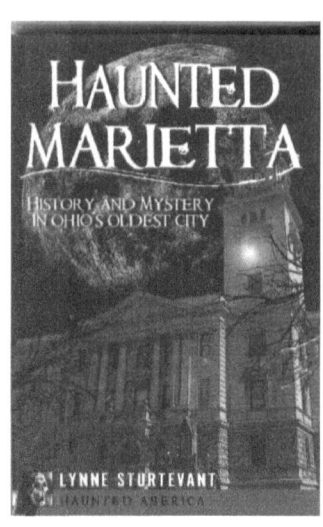

Haunted Marietta: History and Mystery in Ohio's Oldest City explores the supernatural side of the state's first settlement. Visit a crumbling 1835 mansion whose original owner still roams the halls, sit in the plush red seats of an abandoned theater and climb an ancient Indian burial mound. Encounter river pirates, fugitive slaves, an axe murderer, jealous lovers and inept morticians. *Haunted Marietta* delves into various types of otherworldly phenomena, examines the difference between ghost stories and reports of supernatural activity and discusses why certain people become spirits. From an 1815 goblin sighting to a bartender's brush with the unexplained, local author Lynne Sturtevant covers it all.

Hometown:
Writing a Local History or Travel Guide

Many of us dream of becoming published authors. We imagine how it would feel to hold our own book or see it on the shelf at our favorite bookstore. The good news is you can achieve your dream by writing about your hometown.

You can chronicle your area's history. Write about a significant building or local celebrity. Zero in on an interesting neighborhood or time period. Publish a collection of ghost stories or share insider tips and recommendations in a travel book about your town or region.

Hometown: Writing a Local History or Travel Guide is a complete guide to writing and publishing a local interest book.

Topics include choosing the right subject, scope and slant for your book; structuring your project so that you actually finish the manuscript; an honest comparison of traditional and self-publishing options; step-by-step instructions for publishing on Amazon; specific ways to capitalize on local authors' inherent marketing advantages; how to establish your online presence; and how much you might realistically earn in your book's first year and beyond.

www.ingramcontent.com/pod-product-compliance
Lightning Source LLC
Chambersburg PA
CBHW030529220526
45463CB00007B/2760